In the Mind of a
MADE WOMAN

In the Mind of a
MADE WOMAN

JANET BROWN

authorHOUSE®

AuthorHouse™
1663 Liberty Drive
Bloomington, IN 47403
www.authorhouse.com
Phone: 1 (800) 839-8640

Published by AuthorHouse   09/22/2015

ISBN: 978-1-5049-3434-3 (sc)
ISBN: 978-1-5049-3452-7 (hc)
ISBN: 978-1-5049-3451-0 (e)

Library of Congress Control Number: 2015914159

Print information available on the last page.

Prologue

The real growing up after you thought you were already grown…
"A wise person doesn't have much to say, you should have been more observant when Eye was speaking!"

Contents

As A Woman Th{eye}nkith!

Have you ever stopped to
realize what was within?
When you're going through something
does it surface from sin?
You sit and wonder how such
things could happen to me....
It is no one else's fault but mine you see....
You first have to find what's
going on within you,
Then you sit down and figure
out then what you must do,
Circumstances are only brought on by
the situations, in which we permit,
And achievement is the thing that's
received only after you have conquered it,

Life will be hard and there's no
way around the square,
Just make sure that you use the best
formula when getting you there,
Live for you because people will
your neck try and ringeth,
These are just some thoughts
as Janet Thinketh!

Hopeless Me

Here Eye am as an adult and thinking
somehow life would be better,
Eye have my own children so Eye
must get my shit together!
Eye fight so hard to keep my mind
somewhat sane and try not to break,
Eye must strive even harder now
because eye have so much at stake,
Eye leave it up to the higher power in
myself and ask to make it right,
As eye continue to follow the path
in which eye set my sight,
Eye should've known that life would come
with such trials and much tribulation,

Based on my upbringing and
childhood situations,
It never really mattered about the
circumstances neither what went on,
But what has always mattered is just
the road in life that you condone,
But eye can nothing more than
what eye am but sit and wait,
Until eye reach the highest realm of
this earth and my soul may dissipate,
Onto my next journey and
never will ever get to see,
What really became of Janet,
oh that Hopeless Me!

What Happened?

Sometimes Eye just sits and Eye
begin to wonder why,
What is my calling and why am Eye alive?
EYE can't turn to anyone because
the world is just so cold,
In the bible EYE read this, these
are the things that are told,
These days that are upon us
everything shall go wrong,
Nothing will be the same
and how they belong,
Someone please help me and
show me how not to fear,
Tell me how things sometimes clear
up with the drop of a tear,

EYE used to always lie around
and hope to figure this out,
Why are there so many problems?
What's this life really about?
EYE guess all the happiness passed me
by on the days when Eye was napping,
Will someone wake me up and tell
me what the hell happened!!!????

Life is what You Make it

EYE want to say this and hope
all can understand,
If your life is messed up you
should create a plan,
Things spring up without
a moment's notice,
If you're down, then it's
where you want to be,
You're the owner of yourself
so live accordingly,
People talk and say what
they fell they must say,
But people also talk about GOD
then and even today,

It's up to you to change
the lay of the cards,
Since if you live for others
you won't get very far,
If you want to get something
go reach out and grab it,
Tell yourself Eye want that and
Eye am going to have it!
People will be people whether or
not you listen to the talk,
You owe it to yourself to take that lil walk,
Eye've given you now a bit of
knowledge to do what you must do,
Be you own guide, live your life for you,
Don't try to fit or even try to fake it,
Do what you do life is what you make it!

It's Not My Fault

All eye ever wanted was for someone
to love and respect me,
But everyone eye've encountered
appeared to be mentally beneath me,
Eye ask several questions and think
eye've picked up the idea,
That eye shouldn't lower my standards
because they must fight to be here,
Eye used to think and was told
that eye was too over-bearing,
When it seems that eye get approached
by those that are more daring,
Eye come off so strong they say
and have such a strong will,

And eye appear to be detached
when I hide the ways eye feel,
Maybe eye over-access or the
bar's so high in my brain,
But eye've started to feel like
eye'm the one that's insane,
Or is it the world that may
have a problem with me?
Because my standards are set high
but get treated materially,
Eye try to maneuver in this world
just enough to get a grasp,
But this unnecessary chaos out
here is kicking my ass
Eye guess the things in life give you
lessons that must be taught,
Eye am who Eye am and
that It's Not My Fault!

Living Day by Day

EYE tried to live for yesterday but
was told that it's in the past,
EYE tried to live for the future
but now I'm moving too fast,
EYE wish eye could live for today but in
my life so many things tend to go wrong,
I'm awaiting my departure from
this planet unto my real home,
EYE keeps my cool and tells myself you
should look forward to tomorrow,
But every time Eye thought about my
life Eye sunk into a deeper sorrow,
Some out there are worse off so
Eye guess that I'm okay,
But Eye might be able to cope a little
better if Eye starting living day by day.

You Send Me to Ecstasy

Eye love when you send me to ecstasy,

Starting at the top and descending lower,

The way Eye feel is hard to explain,

Because we not only connect

on a physical plane,

With every touch things go a little further,

This place is like no other,

You kiss me in most intimate places,

While were staring in each other's faces',

Now you see it's time to begin,

Going to a place no other has been,

Use What You Have

If you're put down because of weight,
Let it all go; you'll find love
no matter what shape,
Men will try to ignore you if you
don't meet the standard criteria,
Because you lack the face, the
breast and the derriere,
But the right one will appreciate
you to hold and to have,
It's ok if the wrong one
won't take the grab,
If you're within the shape that
the everyone wants a piece,
No one will show you R-E-S-P-E-C-T

Don't get me wrong it seems nice
to say everyone wants a nab,
But if you aren't, learn to
USE what YOU have!

Optimism is the Key

Look inside yourself to
figure out the mystery,
Ask yourself this; why does
misery love company?
Who holds the answers to the
questions that lie inside your fate,
And when the days come will
you make or break,
The decision of the life you live after this,
And are you prepared for
the phenomenal bliss,
Eye want to go to heaven, but
then what would be left,
But what about when you find out
that you are a God yourself,

Look within yourself to change
the world around,
Let people see the true light and
how the "REAL" get down,
Everything around you starts
within you, you'll see,
So remain open-minded,
because Optimism is the Key!

Things Change

Some things may feel as they follow
you your whole life long,
While other things once
there, now are gone,
Those things you held dear to yourself,
But ended up being that of the stealth,
Just sit back keep on living,
watch, sit back and see,
Some of those things were meant to be
held and some were meant to leave,
When you become more mature, you
begin to understand life's' percentile,
Things may become boggled
in your mind for a while,

Like what is this part of your life within
that certain graph and ratio?
But you begin to realize, what
should stay and what must go!
You may never understand why
things happen and even a reason,
But whatever happens you
just keep on heaving,
When you begin to grow you
tend to become estranged,
Just embrace your new beginning
because All Things Change!

Take This Chance!

Read this poem and
understand very clear,
Eye am pure energy, so Eye
am there and here,
Eye tend to understand aspects in
which other's can't seem to relate,
EYE share passion with the world
but also retain so much hate,
Because the people in my life that
Eye loved gave me the blues,
But Eye shall remain me not
matter what other people do,
There are things in life that we
may never understand,

But when we all conjoin we
shall make a Stand!
There are people in the distance
out to stop you and Eye,
But it just helps my hunger grow inside,
Eye tend to ignore and disregard
a lot of what people tend to say,
Because Eye am still me at
the end of the Day,
Regardless of what others do,
You hold your stance,
All Eye'm asking is that You
Take that Chance!

What's to Do?

You said that you loved me and
will always be around,
But eye'm searching for something
more concrete and profound,
If you won't have me and
treat me with respect,
Now's the time to move on, be free and let,
Go of what we've claimed to have
to progress more in our own life,
Tell me the truth do you
really want a wife?
Sometimes eye can believe you
but most times eye can't,
Because the things you tell me
seem to be a bit too bland,

Eye love you with my heart and
eye'll always reserve a space,
But the truth at hand is
what we need to face!
Are we going to be together or
holding to something bare?
Are we still in love or is
there nothing there?
Eye would love to be your companion,
friend and even your lover,
But what eye need to know is that there
will never between us come another,
If you can't promise this well eye'm
only holding to a dream.
And what eye thought of you
isn't what it may seem,
So eye'll end this note now and
give you time to think,

So when eye receive my answer from
you our circle will complete,
Your journey is only for you to chose,
But once you not what you want
then you'll know What's To Do!

Hurt By the Passion

There's this notion but Eye never
seemed to understand,
What really goes on inside
the head of a man?
They treat you all dandy
and yes that fine,
But they tend to live double
and triple lives most times,
Now don't get me wrong Eye'm
not a chauvinist you see,
But Eye can only speak on what
has happened to me,
We accept these things because
he brings us delight,

In actuality You have
always held the Light!
We as women tend to absorb
and rub away all the dirt,
At the same time failing to
remember our own hurt,
Being someone's pushpin, punching
bag or pit to throw old scrapings,
Once you wake up my girl you
won't be hurt by old passion!

Sometimes You Let Go

You know at first eye was not a critic,
And eye wanted love but
never seemed to get it,
Eye thought it would come
flowing, peaceful and free,
Just didn't appear true
when it came to me,
Eye've tried several ways many
times through the years,
And have mainly endured
painful heartache and tears,
Eye had not found a love
capable of loving me back,

My heart is weak, fragile and
filled with repaired cracks,
Eye stay around longer than
anyone else would,
Eye put up with things many
other women never could,
Eye've put so much into people and still
being connected with no progress,
But eye feel that all of my previous
failures were just a test,
There were some relationships
that may have come close,
But the path of loyalty is not
the one that was chose,
Eye should've known better to
expect and think this way,
Cause a boy can't be a man
until he grows up - you say?

Eye'll wait for the man that can
handle a woman such as Eye,
But until then eye can't hold on - so bye,
There's this passage that says
"You reap what you sow",
No need to hold to nothing -
Sometimes you Let Go!

Who Lied?

Who lied and to you they
were more than us?
Who lied and said you must
have a size DD bust?
Who lied and said you have
to run with the crowd?
Who lied and said you had to
be popular to be down?
Who lied and said you
must show and prove,
Who lied and said you can't be U!?
Who lied and said you have
to live up to what "say"?
Who lied and said you won't
get better tomorrow today?

Who lied and said that you have
to live within their band,
Who lied and said you
must buy that brand?
Who lied and said that these were the
rules given and you must abide?
Who Lied? Who Lied? Who Lied?

EYE Confess

Eye confess that Eye didn't
love me from the start,
Eye confess that Eye have a very soft heart,
Eye confess that Eye was
unconfident of myself,
Eye confess that Eye wanted
to be somewhere else,
Eye confess that Eye didn't know me,
Eye confess that Eye wasn't
sure of my degree,
Eye confess that Eye had to
learn that Eye am Mine!
Eye confess that Eye get
confused sometime,

Eye confess that Eye must also
deal with life's stress,
But Eye confess that EYE am
Woman and EYE can Confess!

Caress Me

Eye want to break down a
very sensual ordeal,
About when our souls connect
and how eye feel,
A shadow of a hand to outline
the silhouette real slow,
Starting at the head and
ending at the toe,
They began my lips and
work our way down,
As your fingers slide up under my gown,
You watch my expressions
as you begin to strip,
While sending butterfly
impulses between my hips,

You hold eye contact from the very start,
While sensually stroking my
gallivanting heart,
Those masculine tips glide over my breast,
While eye gently nibble at your neck,
We caress each other unlimited,
Exchanging energy soooo intimate,
That one thing that we strived
for, we did achieve,
Eye love that feeling eye get
when you Caress Me.

How Do EYE Get Out?

Eye have a problem maybe
a circumstance,
No one can help neither
will they understand,
This person Eye've met but
known for a while,
Seems to be in conflict with my lifestyle,
Sometimes Eye'm afraid with
not one word to say,
But must celebrate life every single day,
My emotions are mangled and
Eye'm even distraught,
Cause in life for a long
time love Eye sought,
Love is very complicated a phase,

A very large portion in life it plays,
Eye wake up daily with the
struggle on my mind,
There's nothing relative to time,
You search through space
looking for the one,
Never finding them still waiting
for that day to come,
You let go and let those feelings
come to a drought,
That's the secret to How Eye get out!

Who Knows?

As someone may try to tell you
as you try to figure it out,
What are our real instructions for
life? What's the major route?
Am eye alone in this frenzy
of unresolved questions?
And is everything that goes
on just on big lesson?
Some try to help me but then
again it's all on me,
No one can help me, no one
you see, no one but me,
Sitting here pondering on
what Eye should do next,

In these days you don't
know what to expect!
I look around and observe
what's going on,
But the answer never came along,
Eye just stroll on the waves of life
and follow where it goes,
But at the end of the
situation; Who knows?

A Work of Confidence

Hold your head up high!

Never hold it down!

Laugh and be thankful don't

sit and mope around,

Take pride in yourself, show

it, and let everyone see,

Share with them your

beams of self dignity,

Tell yourself; With me Eye'm satisfied!

Eye'm me no matter what and

yet and still Eye rise!

Live and make progress

please don't be shy,

Look at your life through your

own eyes don't just cruise by,

There is only one you and
you're one of a kind,
Do what's in your own heart but
don't walk through life blind,
So do whatever you feel even if
it makes no dam sense,
Do what makes you happy that's how
you build a work of confidence!

RealEYElization

Eye'm knowing and believe
what all has went on,
If he's sleeping around don't
act as if it's unknown,
My loved one had me but yet
another on the side,
Eye was a good woman and
by the rules did abide,
Eye've been celibate for
about 6 months now,
Eye know that the hurt will
make me stronger somehow,
He's been having relations
with a very close of kin,
But he had vowed to never do it again,

Eye loved so Eye did try to compromise,
But since then Eye've awakened
and began to realize,
That life is composed of a many
twisted and tied situations,
But Eye have now come to
this Realization!

Eye Understand

Some may never understand
the other sex very well,
And maybe that's where most people fail,
Eye'll say it like this because
Eye want to keep it real,
This is really how we all feel,
If there for you well it's and
it's an obvious connect,
But if the tides don't flow then
they become a reject,
You can never predict what
another might do,
So really get to know and understand u!
Make sure that all of your
ducks or in a row,

Because that right person may
otherwise come and just go!
Remember to be who you want to attract,
Or inadvertently pull in a bad batch,
Use your energy and mentality
to be a special brand,
Eye am One so Eye Understand!

Eye Should've but Eye Never Do!

Eye should've listened to my dad,

when Eye was just a little kid,

While Eye should've listened to my mom

saying stop some of what Eye did,

But one thing Eye can say and

it's in every single clue,

Eye should've listened to my

parents but Eye never do!

Eye should've stayed away from the

dark hearts of certain types of man,

Eye should've kept on all of my

clothes, down to my underpants!

Live outside the box, but listen to

me because this world's a zoo,

And you should've read this
poem but People Never Do!
So Eye'll leave you now but with this poem,
Grasp the concept, let it marinate
then you'll show'em!
Oh and let me say this but
this one's the truth,
Never say Eye Should've When
You Can Always Do!

Mistakes

All of us do this but few of us learn,

Somewhere in life we make a left turn,

You try to correct but it seems

to only get worse,

Because it was something that

should've been avoided at first,

Then we turn and point

fingers everywhere else,

When the real person to blame is ourselves,

Eye try and tell myself let go

of what Eye can't prevent,

And only to the higher self

should you be a servant,

But sometimes those mistakes are

because of a misconstrued plan,

But always try to avoid
chaos when you can,
Get your life in check and
just let your aura show,
Wherever there's negativity just let it go,
In your life there may be
several things at stake,
And we have no room for
unnecessary mistakes!

5 Staaaaar Lady

Eye wasn't sure how Eye should

explain my worth but what Eye feel,

Eye'll just let you know be keeping it trill,

Eye have loved me since the

first day that we've met,

Even still some things Eye live to regret,

Eye love me so much because

of who Eye are,

So Eye decided to write in out in stars,

1 star for the love that emulates

from me like a light,

The type of star that shines in

the day not just at night,

2 stars for my independent,

empowering and fun loving nature,

Because without us the world
would be in danger,
3 stars for the beauty that
comes from so deep within,
People don't know how
hard it is in this skin,
4 stars for my beauty, my
glow, and to my intent,
Because Eye know that Eye
am a proficient,
5 stars because most people
consider me crazy,
But in my opinion Eye'm
just a 5 star Lady!

Been Der Done Dat

Let me tell you about a few
things that happened to me,
About how those things made me Me,
Eye fell in love at a very young age,
And now Eye'm unsure in what to engage,
Eye listened to a guy, who told me a lie,
And at my own expense Eye had to cry,
Eye'm a strong woman now
and Eye know that Eye am,
Because my heart is so free because
Eye cleaned up my spam,
My love was locked up all because of him,
But Eye moved on to another diadem,
Life's a hell hole and Eye
was losing my mind,

So stay tuned and updated
don't fall behind,
The years of that shit that
Eye've been through,
Eye feel that no man is a man
for me that will do,
Eye accuse no one but
blame myself for that,
All Eye'm saying is Eye been
der and done dat!

Hopeless Me

Here Eye am an adult and thinking
somehow things would be better,
And Eye have my own children so
Eye must get my shit together!
Eye fight to keep my mind so sane
and Eye try not to break,
Eye have to try even hard now because
Eye have so much at stake,
Eye leave it up to the higher power
and ask help to make things right,
As Eye continue to pray and
meditate at night,
Eye should've known that life would
come with trials and tribulation,

And everyday Eye strive hard
to show appreciation,
Eye assume it doesn't matter mine is
just like any other story you hear,
But wait; No it's not because Eye
something a lot different my dear,
Eye can truly say that my life has
opened up my eyes for me,
Hopeless? Guess not no that's not ME!

Evolution

Someone did ask and Eye
somehow believed,
That we as people are
somewhat misconceived,
We want to come up, but it seems
that we're constantly held down,
So we have this misconception that we
are at no level other than the ground,
We sit here and let others tell
us what we will never have,
And with this idea in our head
we never take a grab,
So until we all stand up
decide on a solution
We will never reach new
heights of evolution.

Eye Don't take Orders!

Aquarius is my sign, which is strong-
willed, independent and free,
But Eye can be none of those
with a lock around me,
Eye start to become aggressive
because Eye can't take orders well,
It's the way that you say things
not the way that you tell,
Most say Eye take too much serious
and Eye need to take un ease,
As once stated earlier, Orders Bitch Please!
Sometimes Eye feel that Eye'm
at the point of no return,
And for some deeper meaning
to life Eye yearn,

When so much evil is around,

seems there may be no escape,

So Eye just retract into my mind,

the one sacred place,

For when inside this realm there

are no boundaries or borders,

Eye will repeat this again

Eye don't Take Orders!

That Life Thing

Sometimes eye just ponder
while in a daze,
Reconstructing the mistakes
in life that were made,
Eye try to think of what eye would undo,
But truth is, where would eye
be without them too?
For every good thing there
must also be bad,
For every happy experience
there must be sad,
For every companion there
be only that one,
No good deed for a bad go undone,

There are things to remember
in life, just to get by,
Like why you should smile
and also must cry,
Eye may be you but have
been through a lot,
Eye've been raped, kidnapped
and could've been shot,
Some give or take could've been
a hell of a more serious,
But so many questions keep
most of us curious,
The L is for life which can be
pleasant or scorned,
The I is for ignorance that is born,
The F is for the fight once
victory is received,
The E for everlasting, my
soul lives eternally,

You can take it from me,

though not a pro yet,

Most of you haven't been

through have of this Eye bet!

Use your chakras to adjust reality

to what you want to bring,

There will never be an easy route

though to the That Life Thing.

Finally

What is this feeling that Eye have

and been searching for years,

Have my heartfelt prayers finally

landed on listening ears,

Eye can't help but smile at the

thought of my new found love,

Eye send thanks to the heavens

for this blessing from above,

Eye've been threw a lot in life and

Eye've given up on my own happiness,

Now Eye have a love where Eye can

say there'll be no more sadness,

It's funny how we met and

began our own thing,

It was through a very peculiar
situation that started as a fling,
Eye'm so glad of the circumstances
no matter how awkward they were,
Now, Eye can say it's my turn and Eye
don't have to worry about another her,
Eye get butterflies whenever Eye think
of you and hear your name,
The love that Eye have accumulated
it should be a shame,
So Eye realized that Eye control
what happens to me,
So it's my turn to be happy
and peaceful Finally!

Sometimes U Just let Go

You know Eye used to not be a love critic,
But Eye wanted love but
never seemed to get it,
I just thought that love should
be clear and free,
Just not so when it came to me,
Eye've tried several types
and for many years,
And have only endured
much pain and tears,
Eye have not found a love
capable of loving me back,
My heart is tired, worn, broken
and full of cracks,

Most time Eye put up with things
but know Eye'm to good,
And a privileged opportunity they
feel as though they should,
Eye put so much in but never seemed
to be matched in progress,
But Eye know that this is all just a test,
There were a few relationships
that came close,
But Eye wasn't the best answer
in the question they chose,
Eye will continue to let my
beautiful light show,
Because them are most times
when you must simply Let Go!

See!

Do you ever feel as though
you are losing control?
Like something is trying to
get out of your soul?
Are some nights scary and
you wake up in a sweat?
Do you know what your purpose is yet?
Sometimes trouble seems to
just come around,
Then you lose the mind that you
thought you had found,
You try not to let the others get to you,
But when they come from all
angles what do you do?
I send up prayers to as why am Eye here?

Then a voice just sit, be easy,

endure and to see my dear,

It's like sometimes Eye think

about my own death,

Why u say? Because Eye felt

Eye had nothing left,

But the beings of my loins help

me to continue to look up,

And not to follow those evil feelings

and thoughts that are in my gut,

Eye have so much to accomplish

because Eye am who Eye am - Me,

Eye will surpass all those things that are

beneath me, just sit back, wait and

See!

Situations

Situations arise that'll leave your
mind boggled and not at ease,
So look around you, pay
attention and take heed,
Things aren't what they seem
and may never be,
Eye've been in this realm for
a while so listen to me,
Eye live everyday and try to maintain,
In my life there are few sunny
days but many with rain,
But Eye can't blame anyone
but me for this error,
But just need to sit down, gather
myself and get it together,

Right now Eye'm just trying to keep it real,
Because Eye've been down in the
valley looking up at the hill,
Eye'm getting it together and
Eye'm well on my way,
Since Eye've learned to take deep
breaths and live day by day,
One day Eye'm bottom low and
then suddenly on top,
Eye know Eye can do this because
it's the mentality Eye got,
Life's punches come in many
styles and variations,
But Eye am Aquarius Eye
adapt to and Situation!

Open

Open you mind to the things
that you must accomplish,
Open your mouth when you
wish to receive something,
Open your eyes to see what
goes on in the low down,
Open your spirit to keep your
feet on solid ground,
Open your heart to the person
you want your life with,
Open your situation so that
you can better it,
Open your ears so that you can
hear what's going on,

Then open your attitude to reveal
inside cause it won't be long,
Open your expectations and
explore the world,
It's only a step away into the unknown
that will cause the unfurl,
Don't stand there wishing and hoping,
Take that leap and always remain Open!

Unusual

Today Eye had a conversation that
was very different from most,
The person that Eye spoke with
had a different approach,
Eye seem to always catch the
eye of a many man,
But none have seem to catch my
attention like this one can,
Eye'm currently involved but
something struck me as odd,
There's a chemistry between us that's
not shallow but more abroad,
He is a much older guy and
Eye guess that's a plus,

Because knowing how to
treat a woman is a plus,
Eye wouldn't mind having a friend
if you're open to the concept,
But Eye don't have time for ignorance
cuz Eye don't want to have to go left,
One day this may or may not
turn into something else,
So Eye'm making more opportune
decisions not only for myself,
For know we'll take it for what it
is and sit back and smile,
To see where this leads us in a little while,
But remember these words
there's no one else like me,
Eye may let you continue
on into my future,
But this is something new to
me, something Unusual!

Make up My Mind

Do you sometimes have things on your
mind that are unexplainable?
Are there things in life that
seem unattainable?
There are solutions to every problem
that you may come to face,
To each individual is
assigned their own race,
No one can help you with yourself but you,
So knowing this information
what are you going to do?
Information you consume plays
a major part in your life,
When all you have to do is follow
the 1st mind don't think twice,

When you think to hard it causes

a dilemma in the end result,

The answer was right there,

but after it you sought,

Your heart tells things that

your mouth won't say,

You want to commit but

are afraid to stay,

What to tell yourself and how

should you really feel,

Am Eye being honest with me

and what's the real deal?

Do Eye know what Eye really need

to have or am Eye confused?

Am Eye being loved and did Eye refuse?

Can Eye say this is what Eye want or not?

Should Eye get rid of what Eye have
or hold onto what Eye got?
Eye've asked for inputs to determine
where my thoughts should be,
But no one can help Make
up My Mind but Me!

A Fool for No One's Love

Someone Eye loved did
treat me bad in fact,
He wouldn't stop sleeping
around behind my back,
No one told me the reasons
why we fall in love,
And Eye still haven't found
one, it's only just because,
Eye had a lot of trust in a love
that Eye considered mine,
And for a short while Eye thought
we were doing just fine,
Eye was misconceived by facts
that were actually fiction,

When Eye lifted that counterfeit
to a king's position,
My heart is so big but has been
twisted, tied and burned,
Now my emotions seem to be a
mixture of a liquid churned,
Eye fly free and awaits my
equal flightless dove,
But until then Eye'm a Fool
for No One's Love!

Mad at Myself

This poem adds a lot to the
many that Eye wrote,
Bout my pride being hurt and
a heart that got broke,
It began with one and
progressed to others,
The breaking of my heart
one after another,
Then one day came when Eye
decided it was enough,
What happened after that made
life a lil more tough,
Eye waited a long while before
Eye replaced the last one,

When you think that it's gone back
around the corners it comes,
It, if you ask a mistake that
can me unmade,
Only if you premeditate the situation
and watch how the game's played,
No one can stop what you allow
to happen to yourself,
Skip that item and put it
back on the shelf,
Switch up the old to try
out something else,
Eye lost out on several opportunities
so Eyr'm Mad at Myself!

Just Because

Sometimes Eye wonder what my
life could really be like,
Eye wondered of the decisions Eye made
going left when it should've been right,
Eye've learned to love myself no matter
what the world thinks of me,
So once Eye transcend this will
all be nothingness you see,
There are things that are obvious
in plain sight to explore,
There are several check points
and invisible doors,
You hold the key to a thing
they call reality,

So what you conjure up is
what becomes actuality,
Look beyond your physical self into the
person that even if you must you drugs,
You must begin to know who
you are Just Because!

Who Am Eye to You

When we started this thing it
must've been all wrong,
You played with my heart and
then stringed me along,
You should've spoken things to
me which were never said,
Because your only focus at the
time was to get me in the bed,
Eye really cared about you and
you didn't understand,
Eye try to be rational and
understand you're merely a man,
Still that's no excuse when you
give someone your heart,

You should've done a lil
better from the start,
That may between the difference
between you and Eye,
Eye've kept it real from the start
Eye didn't have to lie,
Eye know what Eye want and
Eye know what Eye got,
You may not believe me but
Eye do love you a lot,
Regardless to what you've done
and what others might say,
Eye've stood by your side
every step of the way,

Eye believed we had something
that other couples don't,
Just remember Eye'll be there
when other people won't,
Eye've said what Eye've done
and who Eye am to you,
Now my question is Who am Eye to you?

One Day Close

It all started on the day

1981 February 13th,

My mom Janette gave birth to me,

At an early Eye fell victim to

the streets and the game,

Men can't understand women

because our DNA isn't the same,

My knowledge of the world grew as the

streets continued to rip me apart,

But Eye struggled a bit harder to

maintain my book smarts,

My first love came and

messed my life around,

Eye dropped from school, had 2

children, but he had to get down,

Then single with children and
Eye'm raising them alone,
So as a strong, phenomenal, intellectual
woman Eye had to move on,
Eye held my head up and
got my life on track,
One monkey less to carry on my back,
Eye went back to school, got a career,
and multiplied myself by 10,
Eye moved forward and vowed
to never look back again,
Right now Eye'm the one laughing
as Eye sit back and make a toast,
Eye told the world my demise
is never One day Close!

Do You Feel Me

Everyday Eye live my life as
if it may be my last,
And Eye spend my money in
spurts as it's my only cash,
Eye love my family as if they're
the only ones Eye have,
And Eye hold to my man as if
every woman wants a grab,
Eye love my children like Eye know
no one else in this place will,
Eye love myself and if Eye'm someone
with Eye may have to deal,
Eye spread my love for all to share
if you won't accept that's you,

But Eye'll keep living under the sacred
seal and do what Eye must do,
No one can change my goals and
the things that Eye must achieve,
And Eye live every moment reaching
higher than the last me,
Do You Feel Me?

Ecstasy

Eye love when you caress my body all over,

Starting at the top and

proceeding a lil lower,

The way Eye feel is sort of hard to explain,

This feeling that my body

experiences are not the same,

It begins when you enter my mind

and this world we go into,

No outside interferences,

it just me and you,

With every touch things begin

to get a precise bit hectic,

Our souls begin to open and

we let each other in,

You kiss me in my most intimate places,

Watching me closely as Eye
make those sex faces,
Now you see it's this is the time to begin,
So you gently try and slide that piece in,
Pushing further and deeper
and closer inside,
Hearing me make those silent love cries,
Eye love you for what you can
do my soul, not just me,
Cause you send me to this place that
Eye can only explain as Ecstasy!

FED UP

There are many obstacles that
we must face in life,
Most of those struggles are
worth that fight,
And for many of those things
over you have no control,
All you must do is live and let go,
Strive for the things that
you must achieve,
When you get that diamond
you'll be relieved,
For those things that need
that extra punch,
Lay back, roll one up and
smoke dat fat ass blunt,

Think of struggling and life
as the Chess game,
Step up that ladder with pride
and without being mundane,
In life things may get
harder and harder,
Fix that shit and push a lot farther,
Take this shit til you can't take anymore,
Let that shit behind and walk
through another door,
If nothing changes you
just keep pressing on,
Suck that shit cuz, because you are grown,
Take your attitude as if you
don't give a fuck,
It's just how Eye feel when Eye'm Fed Up!

Caress Me

Eye want to tell you about
a certain ordeal,
About when you're caressed
and how you feel,
A set of hands to caress
your body real slow,
In only place where you
and them may know,
You take your time to move across
my skin as my muscles get tight,
Eye lay there stiffened with sensual fright,
You begin at my lips and
work your way down,
As your fingers separate and
slide under my gown,

Your stare fixated on my body as Eye strip,

As you tenderly and steadily kiss my hips,

You slide your masculinity

over my breasts,

While teeth gently pinch your chest,

You explore each portion as unlimited,

Our souls exchange auras and

we become so intimate,

That explosion that we were

hoping for, yes we did achieve,

Eye love the way that we connect

and how you Caress Me!

Anger Beyond Rage

The guys eye meet must have

a certain little style,

No let me say how that

went on a backfire,

A guy eye met at a very young number,

Came in a caused rained and thunder,

Eye felt he loved me but that wasn't so,

And now eye have a different love flow,

Eye may seemed biased

but let me explain,

Eye'll tell some situations without

mentioning a name,

One guy took my virginity

when eye was only a teen,

But eye quickly realized he
wasn't my dream,
Met someone older that seemed
was in a government agency,
Still he wasn't it too disciplined for me,
Met another guy that seemed
to be my closet picker,
But he couldn't seem to keep
his penis out of my sister,
Met another one once eye
skipped to a new state,
But he himself had too
much shit on his plate,
Met another guy that was the first
of a number less than mine,
Don't know what eye got into this time,

But at this point in life it only
matters that eye run the stage,
But all the previous relationships
caused Anger Beyond Rage!

Words of Knowledge

Eye don't care what Eye don't have,

Cause Eye'm happy with what Eye do have,

If these things weren't given to me,

Well honestly they must

weren't supposed to be,

Eye don't care to have what

everyone else has,

Eye can get the highest caliber

of man on my path,

Eye know my level and Eye am

of the highest prestige,

Eye am who Eye am for a

particular reason,

So Eye'ma keep doing me

and keep achieving,

Get a head start and gain
some extra mileage,
A wise fool learns from
Words of Knowledge.

A Connected Lover

A connected lover is one who
stays on your mind,
A true spirit in which you can confine,
One who consoles you when you're sad,
And turns depressing days into to glad,
A connected lover is there
through thick and thin,
Caring, concerned and genuine,
A connected one is there to give a gift,
To give your fragile heart a lift,
When you're down and in despair,
A connected lover is always there,
They do not scold or reprimand,
And they're always there to understand,
If you have that one and that did not fly,

Find that soul before you die,

But if you have your one connected love,

Fall to your knees and look above,

Bless the One and say that prayer,

Now you're richer than a millionaire,

This is one you can bring home to mother,

It's time to hang it up you've

met your Connected Lover.

Emotions

Let's what we can do to explain the
things can make you frown,
These things that make you want
to stay or move around,
You want to let them be but
they won't let you do,
You may do what you must but
these things are always with you,
Emotions evolve within the mind
and purify in the heart,
If you try to hide them they
can turn you dark,
When you're happy they can
make you laugh,

But when you're down they
can make you sad,
These are things to not hold
to but you should share,
Love, joy, peace, patience, goodness,
kindness, self control and care,
These feelings in one way or
another can always help,
To express those things that
you may have felt,
Learn to go beyond that box
and yet remain unopened,
To delve in those things we call Emotions!

How do You Love with 3

It started with me and him
and with my children,
The circumstances changed and
left me in and awkward position,
Eye left myself go and wandered
beyond my boundary,
Only to come out with yet
another adversary,
Someone asked me once a question
that Eye now need an answer to,
That if Eye were in there shoes, in
this situation what would Eye do?
Eye told them Eye couldn't
understand better yet explain,

And that the situation was
more or less insane,
Until Eye got my taste of the
situation about which we spoke,
When one household that was
once one, now became broke,
It's no longer you and Eye
but him, me and you,
Eye only understand how to love
1 and then Eye fell for 2,
Now Eye'm stuck between 2 bridges
and neither Eye wish to burn,
If Eye don't make a wise decision
then it will be my turn;

Trying to be slick and grab-hold
to another good thing,
When Eye already had my
own great King,
Eye never thought Eye would be in
the situation like this you see,
But it ended up being him, him and Me!

MAN

There are some things eye would
like to share about a man,
They will not always tell
you where you stand,
He may never verbally express
the way he feels,
Your intuition should tell you what's real,
A true heart will love you more
than you can know,
But physically that may never show,
But mentally he's connected but
his ego has his pride corrupt,
And his best friend may even try to cut,
There are games that men play when
the woman has an upper grasp,

He wants to hold to tight
but also run fast,
You appear to be too much
but not enough they say,
But you are the reason they
wake up day to day,
Hold on and help him grow if you can,
Because a boy will be a boy until
you grow him as a MAN!

Strengthen Me

Give me the strength and
teach me to lift my head,
Give me the power to surpass
this realm once dead,
Show me how to have peace whether
things are good or bad,
Show me how to spread love
even when my heart is sad,
Spirit lift yourself up above
this earthly life,
Tell me this struggle is not
mine but ours alike,
Teach to press on no matter
what this place may bring,

But keep in my heart forever
this one little thing,
That special universe that is
within your own minds,
Keep pressing upwards towards
that higher incline,
When Eye gain my superior self and
connection with the universe and tree,
And as for now Eye am
continuing to Strengthen Me!

Printed in the United States
By Bookmasters